Looking at Countries

NIGERIA

Jillian Powell

FRANKLIN WATTS
LONDON · SYDNEY

First published in 2006 by
Franklin Watts
338 Euston Road
London NW1 3BH

Franklin Watts Australia
Hachette Children's Books
Level 17/207 Kent Street
Sydney NSW 2000

ISBN-10: 0 7496 6477 0
ISBN-13: 978 0 7496 6477 0

Dewey classification: 916.69

Series editor: Sarah Peutrill
Art director: Jonathan Hair
Design: Rita Storey
Picture research: Diana Morris

Picture credits: Paul Almasy/Corbis: 22. Art Directors/Trip: 4,
26tr. V. & M. Birley/Tropix: 16, 20t. Don Davis/Tropix: 7t, 27.
Eye Ubiquitous/Hutchison: 8, 10, 14. Werner Forman/Corbis:
18bl. Kerstin Geier/Gallo Images/Corbis: 19. Liz Gilbert/
Sygma/Corbis: front cover inset, 18tr. Martin Harvey/Still
Pictures: 6. Ed Kashi/Corbis: 24. M. MacDonald/Tropix: 7b.
James Marshall/Corbis: 23b. Marcel Mettelsiefen/epa/Corbis:
9, 15. Giacomo Pirozzi/Panos: 12. Betty Press/Panos: 17, 20b.
Jacob Silberberg/Panos: 1, 11b, 23t. Superbild/A1 Pix: front
cover main, 11t, 25, 26bl. Liba Taylor/Corbis: 13, 21.

A CIP catalogue record for this book is available from the
British Library.

Printed in China

Contents

Where is Nigeria?

Nigeria is in West Africa. It has borders with four other African countries and a coastline onto the Gulf of Guinea in the Atlantic Ocean.

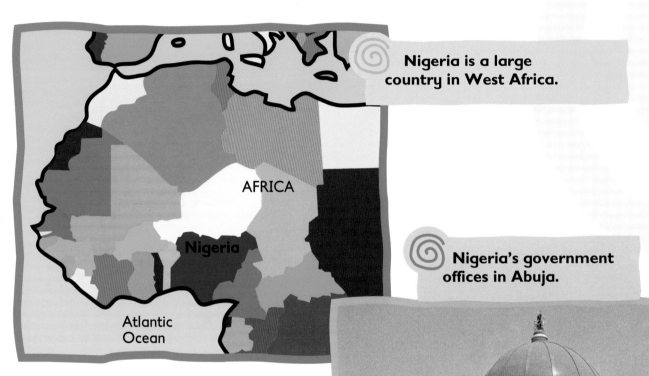

AFRICA

Nigeria

Atlantic Ocean

Nigeria is a large country in West Africa.

Nigeria's government offices in Abuja.

The capital city, Abuja, is in the middle of the country. Abuja is the fastest-growing city in Africa. It became Nigeria's capital in 1991, when government offices moved here from Lagos. It is Nigeria's first planned city.

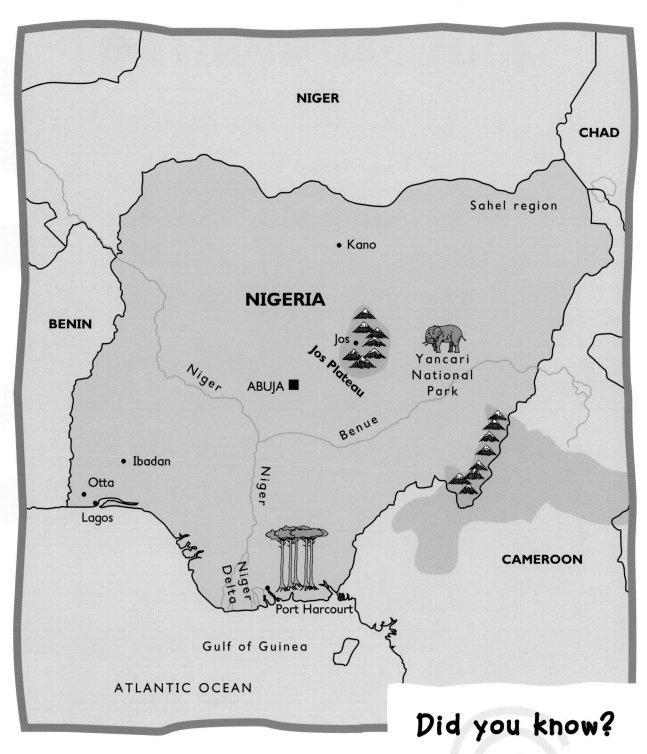

NIGER

CHAD

Sahel region

• Kano

NIGERIA

BENIN

Jos •

Jos Plateau

Yancari National Park

Niger

ABUJA ■

Benue

• Ibadan

Otta •

• Lagos

Niger

Niger Delta

CAMEROON

Port Harcourt

Gulf of Guinea

ATLANTIC OCEAN

Use this map to find the places mentioned in this book.

Did you know?

Nigeria is named after the River Niger which runs through it.

The landscape

Nigeria has a varied landscape, from the flat grassy plains of the savannah to thick tropical rainforest, and salt-water swamps.

Savannah grasslands like this cover much of the country.

There are mountains on the Jos Plateau and in the south-east, on the border with Cameroon.

A dust storm in the Sahel region of the north, which borders the Sahara Desert.

In the far north-east is the dry dusty land of the Sahel region, on the edges of the Sahara Desert.

Did you know?

Sahel is an Arabic word meaning 'border'.

Along the south coast are the swampy mangrove forests of the Niger delta.

Mangroves grow well in the delta region on the south coast.

Weather and seasons

In the south, Nigeria has a tropical climate with a rainy season from April to October and a dry season for the rest of the year. There are high temperatures all year round.

In the central region, it is hot and humid during the rainy season but cooler and drier in the dry season.

The countryside around Zuma Rock, Abuja, in the central region, during the dry season.

Drought means shortages of food and water. Charity organisations set up places where people can collect water.

In the north, it is drier with hot days and cool nights. The rainy season runs from April to September. If rains come late, in June, there can be drought. During the dry season, a strong wind called the harmattan blows from the Sahara between December and March.

Did you know?

Water is precious in Nigeria. Around half of the people do not have safe drinking water easily available to them.

Nigerian people

Nigeria is known as the 'giant of Africa' because it has a population of over 150 million people, the largest of any African country. There are over 250 different tribal peoples that each have their own language, religion and traditions.

Did you know?

About one out of every four Africans is a Nigerian.

The Fulani people herd cows that provide them with meat and milk.

The main groups are the Hausa and Fulani in the north, the Yoruba in the south-west and the Igbo in the south-east.

For most Nigerians, religion is an important part of life. Many Nigerians are Muslims or Christians, and others practise African religions, worshipping gods and goddesses or ancestor spirits.

🌀 **This man is decorating a horse for a Muslim festival.**

🌀 **These Christian women are singing at a church in Otta, on Christmas Day.**

Nigerian children

Many people in Nigeria like to have large families, with six or seven children. Village children play an important part in family life, helping in the fields or with chores after school and in the holidays.

Primary school children singing at morning assembly.

Most children spend 12 years at school and some go on to university, college or trade schools.

These students are learning computer skills at college.

Schools and colleges are now getting more computers, so children can learn the skills they need to find jobs.

But around 12 million children in Nigeria do not go to school. They have to work to bring in money for their families, for example selling water or biscuits on the streets.

Did you know?

In Nigeria, children are usually named on the eighth day after they are born.

Country

Most people in Nigeria live in the country. Relatives from a family often live in groups of houses, called compounds, in the same village.

Everyone plays a part in family life, from parents and grandparents to uncles, aunts and children.

Did you know?

Bicycles are used as taxis in the country. Up to four people are carried on one bicycle!

These people are all relatives from one big family, living together in the same village.

The men work in the fields around the village.
The women look after vegetable plots and
goats, chickens or pigs, and do all the cooking.
In the south, some women earn money by
taking vegetables or cloth to sell at markets.

This village woman is pounding cassava to make a type of flour.

Tribal peoples like the Yoruba and the Igbo
also make pottery, masks and bead or
metalwork to sell to tourists at markets.

City

Cities in Nigeria have grown fast as the population increases, and more people move away from the country to find work. The largest cities include Ibadan, Lagos and Kano. The capital, Abuja, is the centre for government and has an international airport, industries, shops and hotels.

Richer people live in houses behind walls and gates, such as these in Port Harcourt.

Did you know?

Nigerian cities are the fastest-growing in Africa.

Lagos, once the capital, has a population of over 12 million people and is still an important business centre.

Like other Nigerian cities, Lagos faces problems of overcrowding, traffic and pollution. Its streets are often flooded during the rainy season. In the dry season, there can be water shortages, and many people have to buy water.

This street in Lagos is crowded with taxis, buses and people.

Nigerian homes

In the cities, many people live in blocks of flats. The richest people have houses with modern facilities.

The poorest people live in shanty towns, called popular settlements, in houses made from scraps of tin and wood.

These modern flats are in Lagos.

This mud house in Kano is decorated with a carving.

The old city of Kano, in the north, has houses built from mud bricks decorated with pictures. New houses are sometimes built in the old style, but using concrete.

This boy is standing in front of a grain store.

Village houses are built from mud bricks, clay or wood, with roofs made from palm or reed thatch, or corrugated iron. In the swampy delta region, houses are built on stilts to avoid being flooded.

Groups of houses have a grain store and toilet. There is no electricity, and water has to be fetched from a well or pump.

Did you know?

Mud bricks keep houses cool in the day and warm at night.

Food

Food is an important part of family life in Nigeria. Although fast foods are becoming more popular, many people still cook at home for their families and friends. Foods like rice, cereals and spices are sold by weight at local markets.

Discount food stores and fast food shops or stalls are found in towns and cities.

Women and children sell vegetables at a market stall.

Many types of grain, such as rice and maize, are sold at markets.

Cassava and yams are made into flour that is used in soups and stews. These often contain fish, or meat such as goat, beef or chicken. Maize and rice are also eaten, as well as tropical fruits, and vegetables such as peppers and onions.

Did you know?

Cassava, or sweet potatoes, are high in vitamin C.

At work

Oil and natural gas production are two of Nigeria's most important industries. Other industries include food processing, and the manufacture of cement, plastics, car parts, paper, textiles and medicines.

This man on a market stall in Kano is selling cloth made from Nigerian cotton.

In the countryside, most people work in farming or fishing. Farmers have small plots of land and grow enough to eat, and sometimes a little to sell. In the south, there are jobs on large plantations that grow cocoa and groundnuts for export.

A worker checks equipment at a natural gas plant in the south.

Did you know?

Nigeria is the world's 8th largest oil producer, and the largest in Africa.

This is the busy office of a daily newspaper in Lagos.

In cities, many people work in factories or offices, or selling from markets or street stalls. Some street sellers walk along traffic jams, selling goods such as videos and televisions to people in their cars.

Having fun

Football, volleyball, wrestling and boxing are all popular sports in Nigeria. There are also traditional games such as *ayo*, a board game using seeds in cups, and children's hand-clapping games.

These boys are enjoying a game of football beside an oil refinery.

A masquerade dancer, dressed in mask and costume, at a Yoruba festival.

There are colourful festivals all through the year, when people celebrate with feasting, picnics, dancing and drumming.

Some festivals are for the Christian or Muslim religions. Others festivals celebrate African gods or ancestors, or the harvest of fish or crops. Dancers dress in costumes and masks, and there are often wrestling matches or boat races to watch.

Did you know?

Pop music from West Africa is called Highlife music.

Nigeria: the facts

• Nigeria is a federal republic and a member of the Commonwealth of Nations.

• The President is the head of the government.

• The country is divided into 36 states, plus the area of Abuja, the capital city.

Nigerian currency is called the naira. These are 5, 10 and 50 naira notes.

The Nigerian flag has bands of green for its rich land, and white for peace.

An African elephant in the Yancari National Park in eastern Nigeria.

• There are eight national parks in Nigeria. These help to protect Nigeria's landscape and animals, and encourage tourism.

• On 1st October, everyone celebrates the day when Nigeria gained its independence from Britain in 1960. The President talks to the people, and there are parades and celebrations throughout the country.

Did you know?

Each of Nigeria's 36 states has its own radio station.

Glossary

Ancestor a family member who lived in the past.

Cassava a starchy vegetable, also called sweet potato, that grows underground.

Commonwealth of Nations a group of nations that were all once ruled by Britain.

Compound a group of houses that share facilities.

Delta a triangular area of land formed by a river as it spreads and flows into the sea.

Drought a long period without rain.

Equipment the tools needed for a job.

Export the sale of goods to countries overseas.

Federal republic a country or state that has no king or queen, where decision-making power is held by representatives from different regions or states within it.

Mangrove a tropical tree that grows in swampy coastal areas.

Masquerade a festival of dancing, drumming and singing, with masked dancers.

Parade a line of people in the street who have come together to celebrate a special day.

Plantation a farm on which a single crop is grown.

Plateau an area of flat, high ground.

Popular settlement an area of poor and overcrowded housing within a city.

Savannah grasslands in a tropical region.

Swamp land that is very wet.

Tropical within the tropics, part of the Earth lying close to the equator.

Tropical rainforest forest that grows in a tropical region.

Vitamin C a nutrient in food that helps us fight off germs and stay healthy.

Yam a type of root vegetable.

Find out more

www.motherlandnigeria.com/kidzone.html
Children's section of a website written by a Nigerian and packed with information on the country, including stories, jokes and some words to learn.

www.timeforkids.com/TFK/hh/goplaces [Click Nigeria]
Information on Nigeria including a fact file and timeline.

www.afro.com/children/children.html
An African-American website for children to learn about Africa, including key facts on Nigeria.

Note to parents and teachers: Every effort has been made by the Publishers to ensure that these websites are suitable for children, that they are of the highest educational value, and that they contain no inappropriate or offensive material. However, because of the nature of the Internet, it is impossible to guarantee that the contents of these sites will not be altered. We strongly advise that Internet access is supervised by a responsible adult.

Languages

English is spoken everywhere in Nigeria, and is taught in schools. Children also learn French, and another language. There are about 400 different languages spoken in Nigeria, including Igbo, Hausa, Yoruba, and Pidgin, which is a mix of English and African languages.

Igbo is spoken by 18 million people.

Speak some Igbo:

English	Say ...
good morning	ee-bow-lah-chee
good evening	nah-no-nah
how are you?	ee-may-nah ahn-ghan
thank you	ee-may-nah
goodbye	kay-may-see-ah

My map of Nigeria

Trace this map and use the map on page 5
to write the names of all the towns.

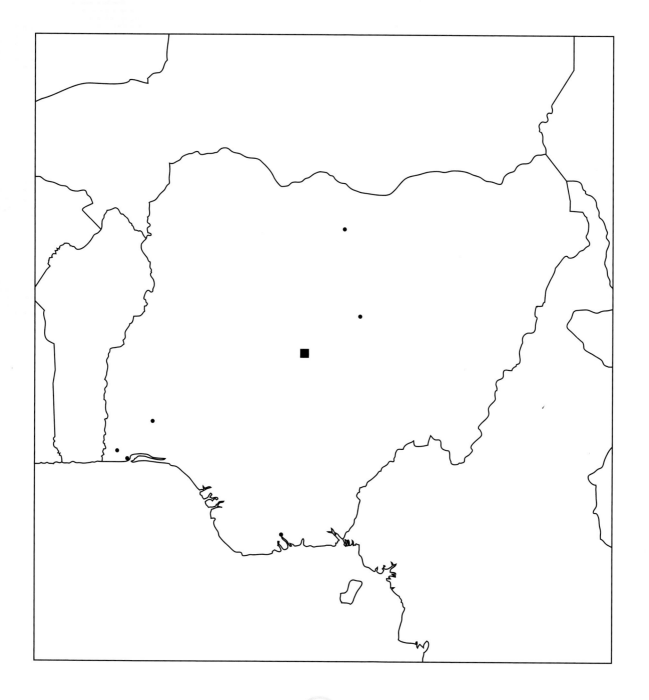

Index